Should Children Be Paid to Go to School?

by Ms. Akin's class
with Tony Stead

capstone
classroom

In our class, we are in a debate about whether students should get paid to go to school. Some students hate school. These students don't give their best effort. Some students love school and look forward to it. These students are usually top-grade students who try their hardest.

There are some students who cannot make up their minds on which side to take. We organized this book to help these students make a decision. We are going to present both sides of the argument, students for and students against. If you are confused like some students, perhaps reading this book will help you make a decision. If you have already made up your mind, perhaps this book will give you a look at the other perspective.

Now we present the trial to you!

The Case for Kids Being Paid to Go to School

I think kids should get paid to go to school because it might ignite a spark for learning! For instance, if they are motivated, they will work hard. If they work hard, they will get good grades. If they get good grades, they know how good it feels and they might change their minds about working hard in school. Then they will work hard and get a good education.

In the future they will get a good job and get paid well. Then they will live happily in a good job. That is why I think kids should get paid to go to school.

by Elizabeth

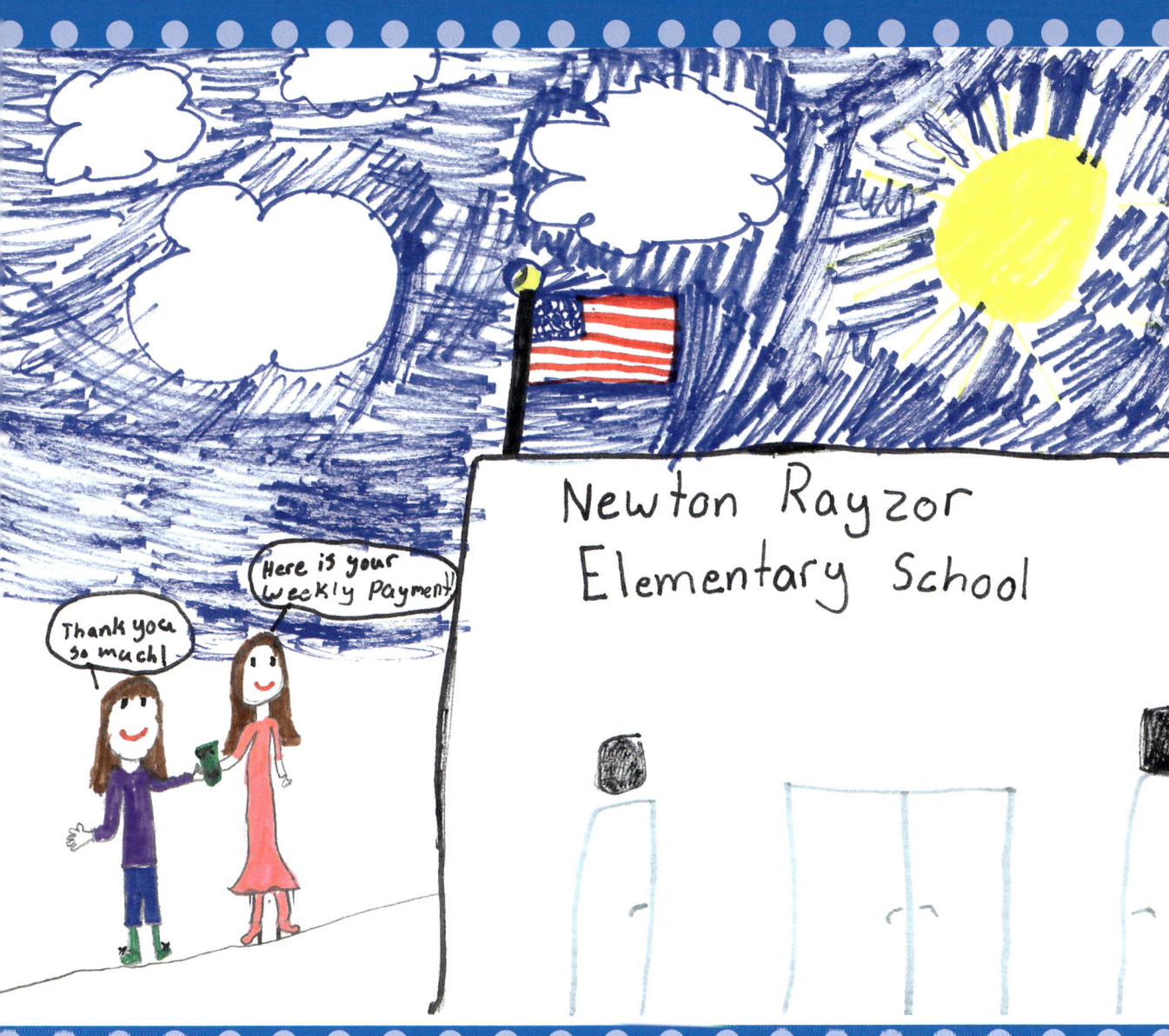

I think kids should get paid to go to school because it would motivate kids to do better in school. Now, I know what you are thinking. An education could help kids get a job and money.

But kids these days always want the same thing: MONEY. It would give kids a better reward that they would consider fair. Therefore, I think kids should get paid to go to school because it would motivate kids to do better in school.

by Josiah

I think kids should get paid to go to school. If kids get paid to go to school, they could save for college so their parents could save money. In addition, if kids start saving in kindergarten, they would be more likely to go to college. For these reasons, I think that kids should get paid to go to school.

by Addison

I think kids should get paid to go to school. Do you?

If parents are paid to go to work, why can't we get paid to go to school? Parents work all day. We work all day, but we don't get paid. I really don't think that is fair. We do the same thing but don't get paid like our parents. I still think kids should get paid to go to school.

by Bella

My opinion is that kids should get paid to go to school because it would encourage them to focus and finish work. This is important because it allows kids to learn more than they would if they didn't pay attention. Therefore, getting paid is good for them in many ways.

It would also help them get more work done, which allows time for more fun things. Doing more fun things encourages them, and working this way eases stress. When kids focus better, the day flows more smoothly. This is why I think kids should get paid to go to school.

by Ethan

The Case Against Kids Being Paid to Go to School

Okay, let's think about this question of kids being paid to go to school. If you ask me, the idea is completely ridiculous. They'll just take advantage by getting paid, and they'll just keep misbehaving. In addition, if kids ARE paid, what would they do with the money?

Finally, I'm pretty sure we all agree when I say that most kids can sit still and focus at school without getting paid. So that's why I think it's bonkers for kids to get paid to go to school!

by Tommy

Without Mo$$EY

(Focus)

We are against paying kids for going to school. It seems like teachers would be bribing kids with money. This is why we dislike the idea. The teachers are the ones giving the knowledge. They are giving us the ability to read, write, do math, and lots of other stuff.

We think kids don't really need money, and by need I mean for living. Kids like money, but don't need it for a living. They don't have to buy their food, their clothes, or their shoes. Some teachers probably couldn't afford to pay all the students in their classes. I mean, it's not fair to all the teachers since they are the ones teaching us. These are some reasons that kids shouldn't get paid to go to school.

by Kason

Do you think kids should get paid to go to school? Well, I don't. I think kids should just go to school for the learning, not the money. The reason I say that is because I don't think that kids will work harder if they get paid.

Also, if they get paid, they would think, "Oh, I got paid. I don't need to work hard." I also think they shouldn't get paid because you would just be wasting money while they weren't working hard. That's why kids shouldn't get paid to go to school.

by Leah

    Do you think kids should get paid to go to school even though they aren't doing any work to help anyone except for themselves? Well, we don't. We think that teachers are the ones giving the knowledge to the kids, so the kids shouldn't get paid.

    Most kids really don't need money because their parents have jobs to get their needs. Some kids might be greedy. Even though they are getting what they need, they want more things. Also, if teachers have to pay kids, they won't have much money left. That's why we think kids shouldn't get paid to go to school.

by Siddhartha

In this book, you have read many different perspectives and reasons about a debate in our class: Should kids get paid to go to school or not?

Here are some reasons you have read for kids getting paid:

- Parents get paid, so students should get paid too.
- It might encourage students to focus if they get paid.
- Students could save up for college.
- Earning money might motivate students.

Here are some reasons kids should not get paid to go to school:

- We get an education, and that is very valuable already.
- Kids would not work harder than they already do now!
- Schools would be wasting money, BIG time.

If they got paid to go to school ↑

If they didn't get paid to go to school ↓

You know what we think. Now, we need YOU to decide. Should kids get paid to go to school? Why? Why not?